Ready and Waiting

Nick Fawcett

kevin mayhew

First published in 2006 by

KEVIN MAYHEW LTD
Buxhall, Stowmarket, Suffolk, IP14 3BW
E-mail: info@kevinmayhew.com
www.kevinmayhew.com

9 8 7 6 5 4 3 2 1 0

ISBN 1 84417 685 4
Catalogue No. 1500944

Cover design by Sara-Jane Came
Edited and typeset by Katherine Laidler

Printed and bound in Great Britain

Contents

Introduction

One theme – waiting – dominates Advent beyond all others, a theme articulated in the ancient prayer: 'Come, Lord, come.' Just as God's people of old waited for the day of the Messiah, so we wait for the return of Christ in fulfilment of God's purpose, for the establishment of his kingdom here on earth, for the final triumph of good over evil, and, ultimately, for life beyond death – overflowing and eternal. Here are the essentials of Christian faith, promises that have inspired, nurtured and sustained generations of believers across the years. Take them away from the gospel and it is left an empty shell, devoid of hope or meaning. Yet, for all that, we struggle to get our heads round these promises, for they talk of realities beyond us, truths that, at best, we glimpse only in part and but dimly understand. How do they relate to life now? Is Advent anything more than a precursor to Christmas, a time for lighting candles, singing seasonal hymns, sending cards and wrapping presents?

In this study book I attempt to answer such questions by trying something rather different from previous courses I've written. Alongside various passages of Scripture, I've also included hypothetical scenarios that bring each theme down to earth and hopefully help us explore its significance for us today in terms of our relationship with God and with others.

First we look at patience – an essential gift for anyone called to wait, and vital both in life and faith. How do we cope when God seems slow to act? How do we deal with those around us when they fail to get things right or their behaviour irritates us? How do we balance living for today with planning for tomorrow?

From questions such as these we move to trust – equally essential in any wait if we are not to abandon it as a waste of time. Is our trust in God sometimes shaken by the way nothing seems to change? What does trusting him actually mean and on what is it based? What should we trust him for, and how can we nurture such trust?

A brief wait is one thing, a long delay another, and Advent speaks very much of the latter. We have no way of knowing when God's purpose will be fulfilled, nor should we spend our time speculating about the future. Faith is about life now and how we use the time God has given us. The third session picks up this theme, exploring how we can help prepare the way of Christ and equip ourselves for the life of faith.

Nobody waits, of course, without good reason. There is always a definite end in mind, and what that is determines how we feel during the waiting. Session four reminds us of the blessings God holds in store for us, the promises that should shape our attitudes and expectations each moment of every day.

If there's a time for waiting, there's also a time for action, and that's the theme of the final session, Advent bringing challenge as well as promise, confronting us with a call to respond. Have we taken that step? Is there more we should be doing? Are we putting things off we'd rather not tackle? Are there decisions we need to face up to?

The beauty of Advent is that it covers past, present and future, speaking through what God has done, will do and is doing here and now. It reminds us of his faithfulness and his promise, and invites us to live in the light of both. Will this book help you do that? I hope so, but, like you, I must wait and see!

NICK FAWCETT

Session 1
Wait a bit – the need for patience

Theme

Waiting involves patience, a gift that should shape every aspect of life.

Opening prayer

O blessed Jesus,
   give me stillness of soul in thee.
Let thy mighty calmness reign in me;
   rule me, O King of gentleness, King of peace.
Give me control, great power of self-control,
   control over my words, thoughts and actions.
From all irritability, want of meekness, want of gentleness,
   dear Lord, deliver me.
By thine own deep patience, give me patience.
Make me in this and all things more and more like thee.
Amen.

St John of the Cross (1542–1591)

Setting the scene

Patience is to be desired more than power; self-control is better than ruling over entire cities. (Proverbs 16:32)

The conclusion of a matter is better than the start. It is better to be patient rather than proud in spirit. (Ecclesiastes 7:8)

Activity

Ensuring there are enough packs of card for everyone, invite members of the group to play a couple of games of Patience (whatever version they're familiar with). Talk together afterwards about why the game is called Patience, and in what way it requires patience to play it.

Introduction

We live today in an impatient world, don't we? We want instant communication, instant news, instant meals, instant service, the idea of having to wait for something being anathema to most people. Whereas in years gone by couples would have saved before furnishing their home or buying a new car, today the majority buy on credit and deal with their debt problem later. Life's too short to hang around, we're told; seize the moment, make hay while the sun shines, live for today. And, of course, such advice is not without merit. We can easily be too cautious for our own good, fears about tomorrow preventing us from fully enjoying the present. If we're scared of taking on a mortgage, for example, we're unlikely ever to own a house. If we're afraid of responsibility, we've little chance of promotion at work. If we're troubled at the prospect of learning new skills, we may find ourselves one day out of a job. If we're frightened about meeting people, we'll probably never strike up lasting relationships. And so we could continue. The longer we wait before taking the plunge, the harder we make things for ourselves.

The downside, however, is that we find it increasingly hard to give things the time they need. Instead of working at a marriage, waiting for understanding to grow, divorce proceedings nowadays seem to be started at the first hint of trouble. Instead of waiting for a new policy to take effect, governments ditch one after another should they fail to produce instant results. Instead of being allowed to grow naturally, farm animals are injected with growth hormones to fatten them up more quickly for slaughter. Instead of planning for retirement, people live only for the present, their only concern to enjoy life now. Few people, it seems, are prepared to wait. As a result we can all too easily rush into a commitment we cannot honour, make a decision we regret, act on impulse only to spend the rest of our life regretting our folly. The old saying 'patience is a virtue' has much to teach us.

What does all this have to do with Advent? The answer lies in that simple word, 'patience' – a theme that lies at the heart of this season, albeit in an altogether different context from the examples mentioned earlier. 'When will God's kingdom be established?' was the cry of the early Church. 'When will the waiting be over and Christ return? When will injustice, sorrow and suffering be ended? When will good finally triumph over evil and love over hatred?' Such questions were not mere theoretical niceties but burning issues that demanded answers, faith itself revolving around them, for whereas Christians had initially assumed they were living in the last days, as year followed year and decade gave way to decade it became harder to maintain such a belief; harder, in fact, to maintain any belief at all, for so much of life seemed to deny their faith.

What was the answer they were given? In the readings that follow are two examples.

Exploring the Scriptures

2 Peter 3:8-15a

Dear friends, don't forget this key point: that in the Lord's eyes one day is no different to a thousand years; they are both the same. Despite what some think, the Lord is not slow to honour his promise. Rather, he is patient with you, desiring that no one should be lost but that all might come to repentance. The day of the Lord, however, will come, stealing upon us like a thief – a day on which, with a deafening noise, the heavens will vanish, the universe be burnt up and destroyed, and the world, together with everything in it, will disappear. In the light of this pending destruction, what sort of people ought you to be? Those whose lives are sanctified, consecrated to God, and those also who not only wait for God's day but also do all in your power to hasten its coming – that day when the heavens will be consumed and destroyed, the stars and planets dissolved by heat. For we are those who wait for the fulfilment of God's promise: the heavens made new along with earth, in which obedience will find a home. So then, my friends, while you wait for that day, do everything you can to be pure and without fault in God's eyes, wholly at peace with him. Consider the patience shown by the Lord to be directed towards your salvation.

James 5:7, 8, 10, 11

Until the Lord comes, my friends, remain patient. Liken it to the way farmers patiently wait for the soil to yield its valuable crop. Just as they wait for the rain of spring and autumn, so you too need to show patience. Keep up your hopes, for the day of the Lord's coming is at hand. Consider, my friends, the prophets who spoke in his name, and see in them examples of patience and fortitude in the face of affliction. We deem them happy on account of their perseverance. You'll have heard, likewise, of the patience of Job, and you'll be well aware of how the Lord finally provided for him. For the Lord is full of mercy and loving-kindness.

Enlarging the picture

Be patient. That's not advice we always welcome, any more than those early Christians would have done, but it's good advice nonetheless. God's time is not the same as ours. We do not understand the workings of his mind, the way he has chosen to fulfil his purpose. We do not know the limits he has set for us, for others or for himself. What we do know is that whatever he has started he will finish, and that, seen or otherwise, he continues to be at work among us.

It's not for us to speculate concerning end times: the when or where of Christ's return or the dawn of God's kingdom. Nor should we lose heart when there seems little if any sign of change, when prayers seem unanswered and hope seems in vain, for the message of Advent is a message for always: be patient. And that applies as much to here and now as any other time, patience being a gift seen as central to Christian discipleship and one of the principal fruits of the Spirit. To illustrate what that means, I want to paint for you four simple scenarios, each leading into points for discussion.

Scenario 1

'We can afford it Chris, I know we can,' said Ella, her eyes pleading for his assent. Chris frowned, caught in two minds. It would be the holiday of a lifetime, no doubt about that, and he wanted to say yes as much as she did, but deep down he knew they *couldn't* afford it. They were up to their necks in debt already, with several huge loans to pay off, not to mention thousands owing on their credit card. It was all they could do to keep up with the mortgage, let alone take on anything else. And yet it was undeniably tempting, the thought of a month exploring the world, lapping up the sun, getting away from it all. Would another loan hurt so much? After all, they could always take out another to cover them all – that's what most of his mates seemed to do.

Ella tugged at his sleeve impatiently. 'Come on, darling, we'll manage somehow. We're only young once remember, so let's take the chance while we can. Tomorrow can take care of itself.'

'But don't you think we should wait a bit?' suggested Chris. 'If we gave it a couple of years we could clear our debts and go then without any shadow hanging over us.'

'Oh Chris,' pouted Ella, 'don't be such a bore! You know how much I want this, and if we don't go now who knows what might happen? You could get knocked down by a bus tomorrow, lose your job, even meet someone else, who can say?'

'But isn't that exactly the point?' persisted Chris. 'We have to think of the future, not simply rush into things. "All things come to those who wait" – isn't that what they say?' The pleading was in *his* eyes this time, but she was having none of it.

'Honestly, Chris, you're hopeless!' she exclaimed. 'If you had your way, we'd never do anything at all.'

'But sweetheart . . .'

'Don't sweetheart me. You're just making excuses. Well, I'm sorry, Chris, but it's time you decided what matters most – me or the bank balance – and I'm telling you this: you'd better make up your mind quickly for I won't wait around for an answer!'

Chris looked at her despairingly, then shrugged his shoulders with a sigh . . .

Discussion points

- We live today, it's often said, in a buy-now-pay-later culture. Do you think that's true? If so, is it a good or a bad thing? What are the advantages and what are the pitfalls?
- What would you have done in Chris' shoes? Do you have any sympathy with Ella's attitude? Do you think people are more impatient generally today than they used to be? If so, about what sort of things in particular? Think, for example, about marriage and divorce, sexual relationships, waiting for an appointment of some sort, even perhaps the way people drive or relate to each other in daily life.
- How do you balance living for today with planning for tomorrow? What do you see as the Christian attitude to such things? Should our attitude be 'This is the day the Lord has made, let us celebrate and enjoy it to the full' (Psalm 118:24), or do we need to be more circumspect?

Scenario 2

Pete looked at his friend anxiously, conscious something was troubling him. It didn't take a degree in psychology to work that one out – the long face and brooding eyes said it all.

'Cheer up, John, it may never happen.'

John smiled wanly, but said nothing.

'Hey, mate, what's up? Spit it out.'

'Oh it's nothing – just a row I had with Harriet this morning.'

Pete couldn't resist a chuckle. 'Phew, you had me worried for a minute – wasn't sure *what* you were going to say.'

'No, nothing too terrible,' said John. 'But I'm ashamed, disappointed . . . not with Harriet, but me.'

'Oh come on,' shrugged Pete, 'we all row sometimes.'

'But this was different,' said John. 'I lost it completely, just snapped. And I'd promised myself it wouldn't happen again.'

Pete nodded. 'So what was it about, this bust-up of yours?'

'That's the daft thing,' answered John, 'I can't remember. It couldn't have been that important it, could it? I just felt I wasn't getting through; that whatever I said to Harriet she wasn't listening . . . didn't even *want* to listen.'

'And she felt just the same about you, I suppose,' observed Pete drily.

John sighed, permitting himself a rueful grin. 'Probably, and she'd have been right, that's the sad thing. I can't change *her* but I can *me*, or at least I should be able to. Only I didn't. I failed again, big time, and I feel like I've let us both down.'

Pete patted his friend on the shoulder. 'Don't be too hard on yourself, mate. You're your own worst critic sometimes. If you can't be patient with yourself, then what chance have you got with Harriet, or anyone else come to that?'

Discussion points

- Does that story ring any bells for you? Are you conscious of times *you've* lost patience rather more easily than you should have done? What caused that and what can you do about it?
- Do you get impatient with yourself sometimes? If so, what about? Are you being fair to yourself? Is it possible you're setting your sights too high, or perhaps not setting them high enough? Do you need to be less uptight in your approach to life?
- What effect does losing your patience have on others? What effect does it have on you? In what ways do you need to be more patient?

Scenario 3

Jane put the phone back into her pocket and looked at her watch again, a hint of doubt entering her mind for the first time. It was ten past eight, nearly half an hour after the time David had promised he'd be there, yet there was no sign of him and no answer on his mobile. He'd come eventually, surely? Or *would* he?

The minutes continued to tick by, and still nothing. Her doubts turned to irritation, anger that he'd not even had the decency to let her know what was happening. Was he held up at work perhaps, stuck in traffic, called away on urgent business? There had to be some reason. But, if so, why hadn't he rung?

The two of them had been an 'item' for a while now, but with David living away it had been weeks since they'd seen each other, and she was aching to see him again. Where could he be?

He'd forgotten, yes, that was it . . . lost track of time for a moment or the date slipped his mind. Only she didn't really believe that; she'd been there when he wrote the day in his diary, and he'd seemed as excited about it as she was.

Nine o'clock came and went . . . well over an hour late . . . and suddenly tears came into her eyes, running unchecked down her face. 'Face it, girl,' she muttered to herself, as she shuffled miserably away, 'you've been stood up.'

A minute later, footsteps thudded on the tarmac and a young man hurtled breathlessly towards the spot where she'd so recently stood. 'Jane!' he shouted, ignoring the startled stares of passers-by. 'Jane, where are you? It's me. I'm *so* sorry. Come back, Jane, wherever you are . . . I can explain, honest . . . Jane!'

Discussion points

- Was Jane right or wrong to give up waiting for David? How long would you have waited in her place? What sort of considerations would have gone through her mind? And what do you think might have delayed David for so long?
- Have there been times when God seems slow to answer prayer or offer help in times of need? Are there situations in which he

has seemed absent? How do you make sense of such times and situations?

- In terms of this world, do you think God's hands are tied in some way? Has he, for example, subjected himself to the laws of nature, or is his purpose thwarted by human disobedience? What factors might prevent him working as he wants to?

Scenario 4

'Robert, can I have a word?'

The vicar turned and smiled. 'Of course, Ruth, what can I do for you? Everything's all right, I hope?'

'Yes, fine thanks,' said Ruth. 'It's just that . . .' She paused, unable to meet his gaze.

'Ruth, what is it?'

'I'm sorry, Robert. I feel I'm letting you down. It's about the outreach project you asked me to take on. I don't think I can carry on with it.'

'But, Ruth,' said Robert, struggling to hide his surprise and disappointment, 'it's going so well!'

Ruth shook her head. 'No, you're just being kind. I know you mean well, and I wish it were true, but it's been weeks now and how many new faces have we seen? One!'

'True,' admitted Robert, 'but it's not just about filling the pews, is it? It's much more than that – about sharing the news, giving people a chance to hear and respond for themselves. And, after all, one person's better than none, surely?'

'Of course, but it's not enough. I've tried, Robert, I really have, but I feel we're getting nowhere, just beating our heads against a brick wall.'

Robert nodded sympathetically. 'I understand how you feel, Ruth, truly, and no, you're not letting me down. But don't rush into a decision, please. Things like this take time – not just weeks but months, years. We have to be patient. It's easy to say that, I know, but the seeds you're sowing may bear much more fruit than you realise. I honestly believe that.'

Ruth hesitated before answering. 'I'd like to think you're right, Robert, but I'm not sure. I guess I expected things to happen more quickly.'

'So, what do you say? Will you give it a bit longer?'

Ruth paused again. 'I don't know. Can I have more time to think about it?'

The vicar smiled gently. 'As much time as you need.'

Discussion points

- Do you expect things to happen too fast sometimes? Can you think of specific instances, either in your life or more generally when you've made that mistake? In what sort of situations do we most need to give things time?
- What are the dangers of looking for instant results? Is there a danger, on the other hand, of using patience as an excuse for accepting the status quo?
- When it comes to prayer, how long will you continue to ask for something before you feel like giving up? How long are you prepared to wait?

Prayer

Lord, when I think only of my own wants and desires,
I am impatient to have them satisfied;
yet in my heart I know that such satisfaction will crumble to dust.
Give me that spirit of hope
which can enable me to want what you want,
and to wait patiently on your time
in the knowledge that in you alone
is found true and lasting pleasure.
Amen.

From the Mozarabic Sacramentary (3rd century)

Food for thought

Consider the following proverbs and quotations. Which do you find most helpful? What are their strengths and weaknesses? Do you agree or disagree with the point they're making?

- Rome wasn't built in a day. (Traditional)
- More haste, less speed. (Traditional)
- Patience is a virtue. (Traditional)
- Make haste slowly. (Traditional)
- Slow and steady wins the race. (Traditional)
- A watched kettle never boils. (Traditional)
- Patience is needed with everyone, but first of all with ourselves. (St Francis de Sales)
- Patience is the companion of wisdom. (St Augustine of Hippo)
- One moment of patience may ward off great disaster, one moment of impatience may ruin a whole life. (Chinese)
- Have patience with a friend rather than lose them for ever. (Traditional)
- A lot of the road to heaven has to be taken at thirty miles an hour. (Evelyn Underhill)
- Do not walk through time without leaving worthy evidence of your passage. (Pope John XXIII)

Prayer

Lord, you're patient with us,
more than we can ever deserve,
forgiving our mistakes
and overlooking our flawed commitment.
Remind us of your great mercy,
and teach us to be patient in turn.

When others frustrate us,
their slowness, mistakes or attitudes testing our temper,
remind us of your great mercy,
and teach us to be patient in turn.

When we're disappointed by ourselves,
dismayed by the weakness of our resolve,
the extent of our faults
and the feebleness of our love,
remind us of your great mercy,
and teach us to be patient in turn.

When we're disillusioned by the world,
frustrated that so little seems to change,
that age-old problems continue,
that human nature seems irredeemably flawed,
remind us of your great mercy,
and teach us to be patient in turn.

When we're impatient with *you*,
wondering why our prayers seem in vain,
why you allow evil to persist,
why life doesn't work out as we hope,
remind us of your great mercy,
and teach us to be patient in turn.
Amen.

Completing the picture

Below are some biblical verses about showing patience. Reflect on them quietly together, and then discuss any further thoughts arising from them.

- Fiery tempers lead to arguments, whereas patience creates peace. A fool gives full rein to their anger, whereas the wise person is patient enough to let it cool down. (Proverbs 15:18; Proverbs 29:11)

- Remain unassuming, gentle and patient. Display your love through being tolerant with one another. (Ephesians 4:2)
- 'This now is what I have to tell you,' declares the sovereign Lord: 'I am establishing an immovable and secure foundation in Zion, a solid cornerstone bearing the words, "A firm faith is one that is also patient".' (Isaiah 28:16)
- Because of his patience Abraham received what God had promised. You also need to be patient, so as to do the will of God and receive what he promises. (Hebrews 6:14; 10:36)
- I waited patiently for the Lord to help me; he listened and heard my cry. (Psalm 40:1)
- Put this in writing, so that a herald may carry it forth. There is still a vision of the appointed time, one that speaks of the end, and it will not turn out to be false. It may seem slow in coming, but wait for it, for you can be sure it will come; it will not be postponed indefinitely. (Habakkuk 2:2, 3)

Blessing

Walk with us on our journey, Lord,
  and touch each moment with your presence,
  so that whatever we do or say,
  think or strive for,
  we may do it with patience,
  trusting *your* timing rather than our own.
Amen.

Session 2
Happy to wait – continuing to trust

Theme

Waiting involves trust, the belief that our wait won't be in vain.

Opening prayer

Trust the past to the mercy of God,
 the present to his love,
 the future to his providence.
Amen.
St Augustine of Hippo (354–430)

Setting the scene

I wait excitedly for the Lord's help, trusting in his word. (Psalm 130:5)

I will watch for the Lord, confidently waiting for God in the knowledge that he will save me. My God will hear me. (Micah 7:7)

Activity

Play together a couple of hands of the card game Cheat, then discuss afterwards what role trust plays in the game and how far you trusted your fellow players.

Introduction

If waiting requires patience, it equally calls for trust. Without this we'd soon lose heart, giving up whatever we're waiting for as a bad job, and, of course, on occasions we do just that. If we've lent money to someone who's a notoriously bad payer, then we're likely sooner rather than later to write it off as a bad debt. If our train to work is late, and has already been cancelled several times that week, the chances are we'll swiftly decide to take the bus instead. Unless, in other words, we've good cause to believe the thing we're waiting for will come, our willingness to wait for it will be strictly limited. Add, however, the vital ingredient of trust and it's a different story. We may have been promised countless times before that the cheque's in the post yet still believe it will finally come. We may believe the young offender will come good even though he's gone off the rails yet again. We may have been let down on occasions too many to number, yet still be ready to wait just once more.

Nowhere is that link between trust and waiting more apparent than at Advent, for the promises associated with this season call for both in abundance. So much in life seems to contradict what we believe, seemingly giving the lie to God's love and testing our confidence in his purpose. Why does he allow poverty, famine, war and suffering to continue? Why doesn't he answer our prayers and grant that request we've made so many times over the years? Why don't we feel as close to him as we should do? Why does the gospel seem irrelevant to so many? Why doesn't the Church grow? Why is good so often crushed and evil allowed to hold sway? As such questions pile up, trust gives way to disillusionment, hope to despair and patience to frustration, the faith of many growing cold.

To all this, however, Advent has one simple answer: trust! Whatever appearances may suggest, keep on believing that God's kingdom will come; that he'll be there when we need him; that his love will never fail or let us go. This is what trust means: believing not simply during the good times but the bad, not just when it's easy but when it's hard. We can all keep faith when there's nothing to rock the boat; it's when the wind blows and the storm comes that true belief shows itself.

Two celebrated passages of Scripture sum up that challenge and assurance.

Exploring the Scriptures

Lamentations 3:22-27

The enduring love of the Lord never fades, his mercies can never be exhausted; each morning they are made new, such is his great faithfulness. 'The Lord is all I need,' declares my soul, 'and so I will trust in him.' The Lord deals kindly with all who put their trust in him. Waiting, then, is the best course open to us – waiting patiently for the Lord to rescue us – and if we can learn that while we're still young, so much the better.

Romans 8:18-25

I regard anything we endure at present to be nothing in comparison to the glory that will be revealed to us. The whole of creation waits with excited yearning for God to reveal his children. Creation was condemned to futility, not by its own choice but by the will of God who so subjected it, in the hope that creation itself might some day be delivered from its bondage to decay in order to share in the wonderful liberty of God's children. We know that up till now all creation moans with pain comparable to the pangs of childbirth, and not only creation but all of us who have received the Spirit, foremost among God's gifts – we groan inwardly with longing as we wait for God to make us his children and set us free. We have been saved by hope, but could we call it hope were we actually to see what we long for? No, for who among us would hope for what we can see here and now? Because we cannot see it, however, we wait patiently.

Enlarging the picture

What, then, does it mean to trust God, and what reason do we have for doing so? The older I get, the more I realise how simplistically we can talk of trust without thinking the issues through, some people indeed speaking as though we can guarantee God will do anything we ask of him so long as our trust is strong enough. The facts, of course, say otherwise, Christians being as prone to life's ills as anyone. Faith is not and should never be seen as a divine insurance policy guaranteeing that everything in life will work out just so. Experience proves for all too many that this simply isn't true. True trust in no way implies that everything will turn out all right or that every wish will be granted. Rather it is the conviction that God's love will triumph despite everything the world can throw against it; that, no matter what we come up against, his strength will be sufficient for all our needs, not even death itself able to separate us from his love.

Is that merely blind faith, a clutching at straws in the face of overwhelming evidence to the contrary? No, says Advent, for the proof of God's faithfulness is the life, death and resurrection of Christ – his coming in fulfilment of age-old promises, his taking the way of the cross, his risen presence among his disciples, his love, peace and strength experienced by countless generations since. Yes, we still have questions, yes, there are aspects of life we cannot make sense of; and, yes, trust is sometimes shaken, but faith is rooted in what God has done and continues to do, in what we have experienced firsthand just as others in turn have experienced it for themselves.

The scenarios that follow explore examples of trust, each leading into discussion of the kind of trust we are called to show in God and the challenges we might face.

Scenario 1

'Are you quite sure you know what you're doing?' asked Mrs Giles for the umpteenth time that day. It was a silly question, she knew that, and it must have seemed rude of her to ask it, for the engineer must have tackled hundreds of jobs like her central heating system over the years, and yet, as the time ticked by, she couldn't help but feel worried. Thankfully, as well as knowing his job inside out, he was well used to dealing with anxious customers.

'No problem, love. Soon have it fixed now.'

'Yes, I'm sorry,' said Mrs Giles, genuinely apologetic. 'It's just that it's taken rather longer than I expected.'

'Rather longer than *I* expected too!' agreed the engineer, with a yet-broader grin. 'That's the trouble with these jobs: they can be a piece of cake or a real devil, and yours, I'm afraid, is the second.'

Mrs Giles' face clouded again, despite herself. 'But you can definitely fix it?'

The engineer nodded in reassurance. 'It may take a bit longer yet, love, but we'll get there eventually. Trust me.'

Discussion points

- Have you had similar experiences to the one above? What went through your mind? Have there been times that caused you to question whether God knows what he's doing? What were these? How did you answer them?
- What does trust in God involve? Do you expect him to fix things for you? In what way? Is this realistic? Is it possible to trust him for the wrong things? Can you give examples?
- On what is your trust in God based? What things most strengthen it?

Scenario 2

Laura rushed excitedly from the classroom and grabbed hold of her mother's arm. 'Mummy, Mummy,' she cried, 'look, I've got some real seeds! Can I plant them?'

Laura's mum hugged her daughter affectionately. 'Well now, sweetheart, let's see, shall we?' She turned over the seed packet to read the instructions, then frowned in disappointment. 'Did your teacher say you're to sow these now?'

'We didn't get them from our teacher,' answered Laura; 'it was a man talking about nature during assembly.'

'I see,' said her mum with a smile. 'Well, darling, we can plant them soon, certainly, but I'm afraid not just yet.'

'Oh *Mummy*!' protested Laura. '*Please*!'

'I'd like to, sweetheart, honestly, but it's not the right time. If we sowed them now, they wouldn't grow, or if they did it would be too cold for the baby plants when they came through and they'd probably die. You wouldn't want that, *would* you?'

Laura looked unconvinced. 'Couldn't we at least try some of them?'

'It's not worth it, darling, believe me. Let's give it a month and plant them then. Trust me, they'll grow much better, and before you know it the whole garden will be full of lovely flowers, and all thanks to you. How does that sound?'

Laura's lip trembled for a moment, only for her to break suddenly into a mischievous grin. 'All right, Mummy, I suppose so. But if it's too soon to plant seeds, do you think it's pocket money time? *Please*!'

Discussion points

- There is a time and place for everything, the book of Ecclesiastes tells us (3:1-8). Do you believe that? Does it help explain occasions when your trust seemed to prove in vain? Can you give examples?
- How far should trust relate to present blessing and how far to future promise?
- What sort of things might cause God to delay answering our prayers or from acting in our world?

Scenario 3

'So let me get this straight.' The bank manager paused and looked sternly across the desk. 'You actually want to borrow another twenty thousand pounds even though you already owe fifty?'

'If that's possible, yes.'

'And tell me again why I should agree.'

The young man opposite shifted uneasily, swallowing hard. 'I know it's a lot to ask, and I admit it seems bad coming back like this cap in hand, but I still believe the venture's a good one. OK, so it's taken longer to get off the ground than expected, and it may take more time yet before the money really starts flowing in, but we'll get there.'

The bank manager pursed his lips. 'Mr Peterson, optimism is all very well, but hardly a basis for handing out yet more of this bank's money. You realise, of course, we could foreclose and you'd lose not just your business but your home as well.'

Mr Peterson winced. 'I'm aware of that, yes, but I'm begging you for just a little more time, *please*. I wish I could give you facts and figures to back up my case, but eventually it's down to whether you still believe in this project, and I dare to hope you do.'

The bank manager cupped his chin in his hands and thought for a moment, then looked up with a smile. 'You're right, Mr Peterson, I do still think this scheme can work, so I'm prepared to authorise the loan, but on one condition: you have five years to pay it back, not just the twenty thousand but the rest as well. I hope you won't let me down. Five years, remember, no more.'

'Thank you, Mr Campbell. Trust me, you won't regret it.'

Discussion points

- In what ways do you demonstrate your trust in God? Do you back up your words with actions? Are you ready to trust him even when there seems little reason to do so?
- In what ways might trust in God involve risk? What sort of investment does God ask us to make in him? How ready are you to make it and what causes you to hold back?
- What aspects of life and faith inspire you to trust God? What things make trust difficult? How ready are you to trust God when things don't work out as you hope or expect?

Scenario 4

'Now then,' said Dr Stone, 'what can I do for you?'

Tessa coughed nervously. 'I'm sorry to pester you again, Doctor, but are the test results back yet? It's been weeks now.'

The doctor shook his head sympathetically. 'I'm afraid not, Mrs Cook. Believe me, if there was any way I could hurry things along I would, for I know how hard this waiting must be for you. It shouldn't be too long now, but I can't promise. We may not hear anything definite for a week or two yet.'

'But you do think I'll be all right though, don't you, Doctor?' said Tessa.

'You know I can't guarantee that one hundred per cent,' answered the doctor, 'which, of course, is why you've had these tests, but I assure you they're only a precaution. If something was seriously wrong, I'd expect to see signs in your general health, but everything else seems fine to me. I can't be certain, and I'd be lying if I said otherwise, but I'm as confident as I can be, Mrs Cook, that you can go home and rest easy.'

Tessa looked down sheepishly. 'I'm sorry, Doctor. I should have more faith in you, shouldn't I, instead of wasting your time like this?'

The doctor shook his head with a smile. 'Not at all. I'd feel just the same in your shoes. Not knowing is never easy. All I can say, though, is what I've said before: try not to worry.'

Tessa rose to go, reassured, if only for the moment. 'I'll try, Doctor, I'll try.'

Discussion points

- Time and again when people came to him for healing Jesus urged them to trust. What do you think he meant by that? What do you see as the role of trust in relation to health and wholeness?
- How well do you think your faith would stand up in times of crisis or tragedy? Is your trust dependent on life working out as you hope or rooted in God's eternal love?
- Do you think God's help and blessing is dependent on us trusting him?

Prayer

O Lord, I do not know what to ask of you.
You alone know what are my true needs.
You love me more than I myself know how to love.
Help me to see my real needs, which are concealed from me.
I dare not ask for either a cross or a consolation;
I can only wait on you.
My heart is open to you.
Come to me and help me, for your great mercy's sake.
I put all my trust in you.
I have no other desire than to fulfil your will.
Teach me how to pray.
Pray yourself in me.
Amen.

Theodore Philaret, Patriarch of Moscow (1553–1633)

Food for thought

Consider the following proverbs and quotations. Which do you find most helpful? What are their strengths and weaknesses? Do you agree or disagree with the point they're making?

- True waiting means waiting without anxiety. (St Francis de Sales)
- To him that waits all things reveal themselves, provided that he has the courage not to deny, in the darkness, what he has seen in the light. (Coventry Patmore)
- Many men have just enough faith to trust God as far as they can see him, and they always sing as far as they can see providence go right; but true faith can sing when its possessors cannot see. It can take hold of God when they cannot discern him. (Charles Haddon Spurgeon)
- God provides for those who trust. (Traditional)

- He who trusts in himself is lost. He who trusts in God can do all things. (St Alphonsus Liguori)
- The more we depend on God, the more dependable we find he is. (Cliff Richard)
- We must wait for God, long, meekly, in the wind and wet, in the thunder and lightning, in the cold and dark. Wait, and he will come. He never comes to those who do not wait. (Frederick W. Faber)

Prayer

When life brings decisions,
and we seek for guidance,
a lamp for our path
and a word to point the way ahead,
Lord,
teach us to trust in you.

When life is confusing,
so much around us seeming to question faith
and to deny your purpose,
Lord,
teach us to trust in you.

When life brings temptations,
the desire to live for today with no thought of tomorrow,
to serve self and forget you and others,
Lord,
teach us to trust in you.

When life is hard,
bringing worry and uncertainty,
pain or heartache,
Lord,
teach us to trust in you.

When life involves challenge,
calling for costly commitment,
distinctive discipleship,
tough choices,
Lord,
teach us to trust in you.

When life brings disappointment,
hopes being dashed
and doors closed,
Lord,
teach us to trust in you.

Whatever life brings,
whatever we are called to face,
in joy or in sorrow,
Lord,
teach us to trust in you.
Amen.

Completing the picture

Below are some biblical verses about waiting and trust. Reflect on them quietly together, and then discuss any further thoughts arising from them.

- Surrender yourself to the Lord; put your trust in him and he will help you; he will cause your obedience to shine like the midday sun. Instead of brooding about how the wicked prosper, their plans coming to fruition, wait patiently for the Lord to act. Don't capitulate to anxiety or anger, for such things will only stir up trouble. (Psalm 37:5-8)
- Those who wait for the Lord will find new strength: they will soar up as though they had the wings of eagles; they will run and not grow tired; they will walk and not feel faint. (Isaiah 40:31)

- When the right time finally came, God sent his Son, born of a woman and born under the law, so that we who were subjects of the law might be redeemed, and, through adoption, become his children. (Galatians 4:4, 5)
- It has pleased him to make known to us the mystery of his will, set forth in Christ – that, in the fullness of time, he might unite all things, in heaven and on earth, in him. (Ephesians 1:9, 10)
- Whenever I feel afraid, I put my trust in you. In God, whose word I honour, in God whom I trust; I will not fear, for what can flesh do to me? The Lord is a bastion for the oppressed, a source of strength in times of trouble. All who revere your name, Lord, place their trust in you, for you have never abandoned those who seek you. (Psalm 56:3, 4; 9:9, 10)
- I trust in you, Lord. I say, 'You are my God; my times are in your hand. (Psalm 31:14, 15a)
- Let us unswervingly hold fast to the hope we profess, for we trust God to honour his promise. (Hebrews 10:23)

Blessing

Whether we trust you or whether we don't,
whether life's easy or whether it's hard,
go with us, Lord,
and keep us in the palm of your hand,
until that day when everything hidden is revealed,
everything imperfect made new,
and we rejoice in your love for ever.
Amen.

Session 3
Ready and waiting – prepared to sit it out

Theme

Waiting involves being prepared for a delay, and doing all we can to be ready to grasp what we're waiting for when it finally arrives.

Opening prayer

Help me, Lord,
  always to wait for you,
  to wish for you
  and to watch for you,
  so that at your coming you may find me ready.
For your sake I ask it.
Amen.

Author unknown

Setting the scene

We wait, though, for the new heavens and earth that God has promised, where righteousness will be at home. So then my friends, endeavour as you wait for that day to be pure and without fault in God's eyes, fully at peace with him. As our dear friend Paul, in his God-given wisdom said when he wrote to you, regard our Lord's patience as providing you with the opportunity of securing salvation. (2 Peter 3:13-15)

As for you my friends, continue to build yourselves up in your most blessed faith. Pray in the Spirit's power, and remain within the love of God, as you wait for our Lord Jesus Christ in his mercy to grant you eternal life. (Jude: 20, 21)

Activity

Play together a hand of the card game Rummy. Chat informally afterwards about what cards people were waiting for, and in what ways they were preparing to go out or to reduce their score should someone else go out (for example, changing tack midway, discarding high-scoring cards). Does a game as simple as this have anything to teach us about life?

Introduction

Anyone who's sat patiently in a benefit office, railway station or hospital waiting room will know how frustrating an experience it can be, to the point that we give up waiting altogether. Five minutes is all right, ten minutes, even half an hour, but when it goes beyond that we understandably grow restless, and rightly so. None of us like to wait longer than is absolutely necessary – a fact reflected in the introduction of measures designed to prevent this, such as the so-called 'Patients' Charter'.

Sometimes, though, waiting is an inevitable fact of life. Queues will form, for example, for a massively popular event, only those who are ready to wait the longest being guaranteed entry. Court cases, building projects and the like may take years before they're finished, a garden decades to mature, and a disease still longer to be eradicated, and so we could continue. In numerous areas of life we must be prepared for a long wait before we can expect results.

Partly, of course, this brings us back to patience, but a lengthy delay calls for rather more than that. If we're not swiftly to lose heart, we need to prepare ourselves for such moments, and to use the time spent waiting wisely, not only to ensure it isn't in vain but also to be ready to grasp whatever it is we're waiting for when it finally materialises. To return, for example, to eradicating a disease, scientists and researchers don't simply sit back and wait for it to happen – if they did that, they'd be waiting for ever. Instead they study, experiment, conduct trials and so forth. And when, finally, they come up with the drug, vaccine or treatment required, there is a pharmaceutical and medical network in place to ensure that their efforts will not have been in vain. Waiting, in other words, involves action.

There's more still. To pursue the analogy further, scientists, like those in any other discipline, do not simply sit on their laurels, complacently believing they know all there is to know. They recognise the importance of staying up to date with recent research, and so make time for what's come to be called 'Continuing Professional Development'. Even the greatest experts in a given field would soon be of little use if they spent a number of years away, entirely removed from their job. Skills and understanding constantly need to be refreshed if they are to be up to the task required of them.

Once again, there's a parallel here with Advent, for as Christians we are not called simply to sit back and wait for the dawn of God's kingdom. We have a part to play in working for its coming, together with a responsibility to use the time God has given to prepare ourselves for it. The present, then, is as important as the future; indeed, far from dwelling on what is yet to be, we need to focus on life now, allowing it to be shaped by the future God has promised and consecrating it to him in consequence. That was the lesson learned in the early Church as Christians came to understand that God's kingdom wasn't as imminent as they'd imagined. Faith, they realised, is as much about today as tomorrow, as much about helping us live in the world here and now as anticipating what might be, as much about glimpsing God in his broken creation as in the new heaven and earth he holds in store.

The readings that follow may appear, at first sight, to give the opposite impression, each seeming concerned chiefly with end times, but look more carefully and you'll see otherwise.

Exploring the Scriptures

Luke 12:35-40

Be prepared for whatever may come, kitted out for action and with lamps lit, as though you were servants waiting for your master to return from a wedding reception. Should he arrive and knock at the door, such servants would be ready to open it to him immediately. And how glad will those be whom their master finds awake and ready to welcome him on his return. He'll take his coat off, I tell you, invite them to relax, and wait on them. Provided he finds them prepared, even if it be at midnight or into the small hours, how happy they will be. Similarly, you can guarantee that a householder would prevent a thief breaking into his house if he knew what time the break-in was intended. You, then, in turn, must be ready, because the coming of the Son of Man will be at a time you do not expect.

Matthew 25:1-13

When the time comes the kingdom of heaven will be like this. There were once ten young women – five foolish and five wise – who, taking up their oil lamps, went out to meet the bridegroom. The foolish women remembered their lamps but forgot to take any reserves of oil with them, whereas the wise filled containers with spare oil for their lamps.

The bridegroom's coming being delayed, the women's heads began to nod and they were soon asleep. It had reached midnight before the cry rang out, 'The bridegroom's approaching! Come and greet him!', whereupon the ten young women awoke and started to trim their lamps. 'Lend us some oil,' the foolish ones asked of the wise, 'or our lamps will go out.' 'Certainly not!' came the reply. 'There's not enough for you as well as us. Go to the shop and buy some yourselves.' So off went the foolish women to buy some oil; but while they were away the bridegroom arrived. Those five who remained went in with him to the wedding banquet, the door being firmly closed behind them. 'Sir, sir,' begged the others when they returned, 'let us in!' 'Definitely not,' answered the bridegroom. 'I've no idea who you are.' 'Watch out, then,' warned Jesus, 'because you do not know the day or hour.'

Enlarging the picture

We wait for the day of Christ's coming and the dawn of God's kingdom – that is the heart of the Christian message, a vision of the future inspiring us in the present. But the concern in both of those passages is with being ready now; preparing ourselves for that day, no matter how long it might take. Instead of encouraging speculation about dates and times, the emphasis is firmly upon how we live in the present.

In what ways, then, can we and should we prepare ourselves to wait for what God holds in store? In the following four scenarios, together with associated discussion points, I hope, with your help, to tease that out.

Scenario 1

'Can I help you?' asked the receptionist.

'Yes, the name's Mackenzie – John Mackenzie. Is there are any chance I could see Mr Hart?'

'Um, do you have an appointment?'

'No, I'm afraid not. It's about my court case next month. I've just received more information.'

'I see. Well, he's very busy at the moment but if you're prepared to wait, he may be able to fit you in later.'

'That's fine.'

The receptionist looked again at the appointments list, and her brow furrowed. 'You could be in for a long wait, you know – several hours possibly. Are you sure you wouldn't prefer to make an appointment for next week?'

'No, I'm happy to wait, if that's OK.'

'All right, Mr Mackenzie, would you take a seat and I'll let you know as soon as we have a space.'

Discussion points

- What sort of things in life need time before we can expect results? Have there been occasions when you've missed out on something because you failed to wait long enough?
- When you became a Christian, did you expect instant results? If so, in what way (for example, God to answer certain prayers or help you change overnight)? Did these materialise?
- Are there ways in which, as a Christian, having to wait for things has helped you? Could you enlarge on this? What aspects of Christian discipleship need time to develop?

Scenario 2

'So, Mr Stead, you're looking to invest your money.'

'That's right. It seems daft just leaving it in the bank account, but I'm not quite sure how best to use it. Could you give me some ideas?'

'Certainly. It depends really on how long you're happy to tie your money up for – and, of course, on how much you want to invest. Give it five years and obviously the room for growth is limited, but if you're ready to wait longer for a return – say, twenty to twenty-five years – then it's a different story. You could do very nicely indeed. Essentially, the more time you're willing to give it, the more you can hope to get out at the end.'

'Sounds reasonable, but what happens if I have to withdraw early?'

'Ah, well, that's the problem. In any investment much of the profit accumulates in the later years so if you cash in early, you could be in for a disappointment. For maximum returns you need to be ready for the long haul, I'm afraid. If you've any doubts on that score, then I'd urge you to go for something shorter term.'

'No, it shouldn't be a problem. Let's say twenty-five years, shall we? What sort of profit might I be talking about?'

'Well now, let's see. I think we could find something very useful for that . . . very useful indeed . . .'

Discussion points

- It's sometimes said that we get out of life what we put into it. How far do you think that's true? Could the same be said of our relationship with God? If so, in what way?
- Do you put as much into your relationship with God as you should do and as you once did? What holds you back from doing more?
- Do you see discipleship primarily in terms of what you get out of it or in terms of what you can put in?

Scenario 3

'Heavens, you're loaded up! Where are you off to – a camping holiday?'

'Not exactly.'

'Staying with friends, then?'

'No, we're off to Wimbledon, actually. It's the start of the tennis next week, and we're determined to get tickets. We've tried for the last few years but always been too far back in the queue, even though we camped out overnight. This time we're ready for two nights, perhaps even three.'

'Wow! That must take a bit of organising!'

'You're telling me! It's not just the food and stuff, but silly little things like having a wash, nipping to the loo and so on. It all has to be planned – almost like a military operation – but it's worth it.'

'So you reckon you'll get in this year?'

'I hope so.'

'And if you don't?'

'Then I guess we'll just have to try again next time. We'll camp out for a week if necessary – however long it takes.'

Discussion points

- It's an old chestnut, but if Christ were to return tomorrow, how ready would you be to greet him? What could and should you be doing to prepare yourself in terms of building up your faith, growing in Christian maturity?

- The Apostle Paul speaks of putting on the armour of God (Ephesians 6:11-18a; see *Completing the picture* – page 43). What does he mean by that, and how far do you do it?
- What stands in the way of the above? Which aspects do you find most difficult and what can you do about it?

Scenario 4

'Mum, guess what? I've been picked for the county athletics team!'

'Tom, that's wonderful news! Well done *you*!'

'It's great, isn't it! Wow, I can hardly wait.'

'So when's it to be?' asked his mother.

'Oh, not for months yet – 30 August.'

'It'll soon come.'

'Not soon enough, though,' said Tom. 'What can I do with myself in the meantime, Mum?'

His mother smiled. 'You know full well the answer to that: train, train and train again.'

'Oh, *Mum*!' groaned Tom. 'Do I have to?'

'You don't *have* to, no, but if you're hoping to win anything, then the answer's yes. And if you're serious about reaching the top, then you'd better get used to the idea pretty quickly, for it won't come through sitting about waiting. You've got to prepare yourself so that when the opportunity comes you're ready to take it.'

Tom grimaced. 'Maybe it's not such a good idea after all.'

'You don't mean that, Tom!' exclaimed his mother.

'No, only kidding.'

'I should hope so. Oh, by the way, have you tidied your room yet?' She looked up, then spun round in surprise as she caught sight of Tom hurrying outside.

'Tom?'

'Sorry, Mum, no time to stop,' he called back. 'Must keep up the training, you know!'

Discussion points

- We talk as Christians about commitment and so forth, but how high does your faith rank in your list of priorities? How much time do you give it? Does the way you live back up your answer?
- In what ways here and now can the Church work for the growth of God's kingdom? What is *your* church doing? What are *you* doing?
- What do you think it means to help prepare the way of Christ? How far does your faith in the future influence the way you live and act in the present?

Prayer

Lord Jesus Christ, pierce my soul with your love
so that I may always long for you alone,
who are the bread of angels
and the fulfilment of the soul's deepest desires.
May my heart always hunger and feed upon you,
so that my soul may be filled with the sweetness of your presence.
May my soul thirst for you,
who are the source of life, wisdom, knowledge, light
and all the riches of God our Father.
May I always seek and find you,
think upon you,
speak to you
and do all things for the honour and glory of your holy name.
Be always my only hope,
my peace, my refuge and my help
in whom my heart is rooted
so that I may never be separated from you.
Amen.

St Bonaventure (1221–1274)

Food for thought

Consider the following proverbs and quotations. Which do you find most helpful? What are their strengths and weaknesses? Do you agree or disagree with the point they're making?

- He who neglects the present moment throws away all he has. (Schiller)
- Time is full of eternity. As we use it so shall we be. (Henry Manning)
- The most effective way to ensure the value of the future is to confront the present courageously and constructively. (Rollo May)
- The sole purpose of life in time is to gain merit for life in eternity. (St Augustine of Hippo)
- We have all eternity to celebrate our victories, but only one short hour before sunset in which to win them. (Robert Moffat)

Prayer

You have given us time, Lord,
to grow in faith,
learn more of you
and experience more of your love and mercy.
Teach us to appreciate your gift
and to use it wisely.

You have given us time to serve you,
to show our faith in word and deed,
loving as you have loved us.
Teach us to appreciate your gift
and to use it wisely.

You have given us time to speak of you,
to testify to all you have done

and witness to your renewing power.
Teach us to appreciate your gift
and to use it wisely.

You have given us time to worship you,
to acknowledge your goodness,
celebrate your grace
and declare your praise.
Teach us to appreciate your gift
and to use it wisely.

You have given us time to live,
to delight in your countless gifts,
rejoice in the beauty of this world,
exult in your many blessings.
Teach us to appreciate your gift
and to use it wisely.

You have given us time to prepare,
not just for the days ahead but for all eternity,
for the new life and untold joys you hold in store.
Teach us to appreciate your gift
and to use it wisely.
Amen.

Completing the picture

Spend a few moments mulling over the following passages, reflecting on what they add to the points already discussed:

- Don the whole armour of God, so that you may be able to withstand the ruses of the devil. For we do battle not with flesh and blood but with the rulers, authorities and cosmic powers of darkness – with the spiritual forces of evil in high places. Take up the whole armour of God, so that, having done everything, you may be able to resist and stand resolute on that evil day. Stand, therefore, and secure the belt of truth around your waist, and put on the breastplate of righteousness. Shoe your feet with a readiness to proclaim the gospel of peace. Above all, grasp the shield of faith, with which you will be able to smother the flaming arrows of the evil one. Take also, by prayer and supplication, the helmet of salvation, and the sword of the Spirit, which is the word of God. (Ephesians 6:11-18a)

- Do you not know that of all those running in a race only one receives the prize? Run, therefore, so that you may be the one who obtains it. Athletes wrestle to discipline their bodies, so that they may receive an award that ultimately perishes, but we strive for an imperishable award. In consequence, I do not run aimlessly, nor do I box as though I am pummelling thin air, but I subject my body to punishment to make sure that, having announced the race to others, I am not disqualified from it myself. (1 Corinthians 9:24-27)
- A voice cries out: 'Prepare in the wilderness the way of the Lord, make straight a highway for our God in the desert.' (Isaiah 40:3)
- May you be fortified with all the strength that emanates from his awesome power, so that, come what may, you can patiently endure it. (Colossians 1:11)
- I want to know Christ, and the power of his resurrection, and the fellowship with him that comes through sharing his suffering, even identifying with his death. Not that I have yet received these or been made perfect, but I follow Christ so that I may take hold of them, even as Christ has taken hold of me. (Philippians 3:10, 12)
- May God, the fount of all patience and encouragement, help you to share a common mind by emulating the example of Jesus Christ, so that collectively and with one accord you may praise the God and Father of our Lord Jesus Christ. (Romans 15:5, 6)

Blessing

Go with us now, Lord,
  and help us to consecrate every moment
  and every aspect of our lives
  to you.
Equip us to know and love you better,
  so that we may be ready to serve you now
  and to celebrate that day
  when your kingdom comes in all its glory.
Amen.

Session 4
Wait and see – expecting the best

Theme

Waiting involves expectation, the conviction that our wait will prove worth it.

Opening prayer

O Christ, our Morning Star,
Splendour of Light Eternal,
shining with the glory of the rainbow,
come and waken us from the greyness of our apathy
and renew in us your gift of hope.
Amen.

The Venerable Bede (671–753)

Setting the scene

I wait for the Lord with more eagerness than those on sentry duty long for sunrise, than those on night patrol anticipate the dawn. (Psalm 130:6)

No eye has seen, nor ear heard, nor any heart conceived of the things that God has prepared for those who love him. (1 Corinthians 2:9)

Activity

Play together a game of Picture Lotto or something similar. After someone has won, talk together about what people were waiting for, how near they got and whether or not they expected to win. Invite informal discussion about times when people's hopes were dashed or realised.

Introduction

Our attitude towards waiting and our willingness to wait depends very much on what we're waiting for. If we're standing outside the boss's office waiting for a dressing-down, or sitting at the dentist's waiting for an extraction, then we'll probably be waiting with trepidation, desperately wishing that the moment might never come. If, though, we're waiting for a holiday, a treat or some other special occasion, then our feelings are altogether different. We look forward with excitement, eagerly counting down the months, weeks, days; whatever it is we're waiting for can scarcely come soon enough. Instead of dread there's anticipation, instead of resignation, hope, and though the waiting may seem for ever, we're more than happy to stick with it, confident it will be worth the wait. Instead of blighting the present, the thing waited for transforms it, bringing joy, hope, expectancy and purpose.

So it is also with Advent, for this is a season that speaks of both present and future, of life to come shaping life now. We look forward to a new heaven and earth, a time when there will be no more sorrow and suffering, no more darkness and death. We anticipate blessings too wonderful to contemplate. We wait for that day when we will see in full rather than in part, when we will know even as we are fully known, when we will enter into the joy of our Father's kingdom. And in all this we see reason to celebrate here and now, to expect fulfilment in this life as well as in the life to come, to believe God delights and desires to grant us his blessing.

The following two passages give just a taste of that expectation we are called to share.

Exploring the Scriptures

Philippians 3:20, 21

We, however, are citizens of heaven and eagerly await the coming from heaven of our Saviour, the Lord Jesus Christ, who, through that power with which he is able to subject all things to his authority, will transform our feeble human bodies, fashioning them into the likeness of his own glorious body.

Revelation 21:1, 3-5

Then I saw a new heaven and earth, the first having passed away, and there was no longer any sea. And I heard a voice booming from heaven, declaring, 'Look, God has made his home among humankind. He will live among them and they will be his people, and he himself will be with them, wiping all tears from their eyes. There will be an end to death, to sorrow, weeping and pain – all these will be no more, for former things will have passed for ever.'

Enlarging the picture

Those words are but some of the many in Scripture speaking of our hope in Christ. But in what way should such promises shape the present? Should we focus our thoughts, as some do, on end times and the return of Christ, speculating on how and when this might come? Should we see this life as a means to an end, a stepping stone on the road to heaven? Or should our sense of expectation spill over into daily life, giving a sense of promise to each day and moment? To put it more simply, where and when should we expect God's blessings?

The testimony of Scripture strongly suggests that it's a question of 'both/and' rather than 'either/or'. Ultimately, our hope lies beyond this world in what at present we can barely imagine, let alone grasp. Our talk of God's kingdom and eternal life is necessarily sketchy, for these relate to an otherworldly dimension glimpsed by faith rather than sight. But our confidence in these promises rests in what we have experienced and understood: in peace that passes understanding, in the assurance of forgiveness, in irrepressible joy bubbling up within, in the strength, inspiration, help and guidance we have so constantly received. On that basis we are able to greet each day with hope in our hearts, confidently anticipating all that it may hold.

The scenarios that follow explore in more detail just what such expectation might mean, each leading on to points for discussion.

Scenario 1

Justin looked eagerly at the collection of bags his mother brought in from the car.

'Are those my Christmas presents?' he asked, eyes alight with curiosity.

'Possibly,' said his mum, doing her best to hide them. 'Wait and see.'

Justin sidled closer, inquisitive fingers reaching out to touch.

'Hey, hands off! They're meant to be a surprise, you know.'

'Oh, Mum,' protested Justin. 'Can't I even have a peek?'

'Certainly not.'

'All right, give us a clue, then.'

'No, it would spoil your Christmas.'

'It wouldn't.'

'Yes, it would. Anyway, you might not like what I've bought.'

Justin looked worried for a moment. He hadn't considered that possibility. But then he caught the note of laughter in his mother's voice.

'Oh, go on, Mum, tell me what you've bought, *please*.'

His mother gave an exasperated sigh. 'Listen, Justin, I've told you once and I'll tell you again. You'll just have to wait and see, and that's an end to it.'

Discussion points

- Waiting for something can be as special as actually receiving it. Do you think that's true? If so, in what way? Can you give examples?

- What do you expect or hope for from God? Do you ask him in prayer to grant what you wish or to do what *he* wishes?
- Do you see God as one who holds good things in store? If so, in what way? Do you see those blessings as conditional? Once again, if so, in what way?

Scenario 2

'Do you really think you can do something with this?' Tom asked as he looked out across the derelict garden, doubt written into his eyes.

The garden designer grinned. 'Sure, no problem.'

'But it's a wilderness,' sighed Tom, 'just look at it! I've never seen such a tangle of weeds and rubbish. Quite honestly, I wouldn't know where to begin.'

'It's a challenge, certainly,' acknowledged the designer, 'but you'll be surprised what we can do. It won't happen overnight, of course, and even when it's finished it will take months to mature fully, but, believe me, in time you won't recognise it. Here, take a look at these plans I've drawn up.'

Tom looked at the drawings wide-eyed with astonishment. 'These are the wrong plans, surely?' he said finally. 'You can't possibly create anything so beautiful out of a jungle like this!'

'I thought you'd like it.'

'*Like* it!' exclaimed Tom. 'I *love* it!' But are you serious? You really think you can do it?'

'Oh yes,' said the designer. 'You just wait and see.'

Discussion points

- Have you experience of people, places or situations in which there have been astonishing changes? Can you give examples? What surprised you most? What made these changes possible? And how much time was needed to effect the transformation?
- Do you still have a sense of what God is able to do in your life? Do you still truly believe that the way of Christ can make an impact on the world?

- In what ways has God already changed you? And in what ways has he changed the world?

Scenario 3

'Hey, Liz, what's up? You look so worried.'

'I am, Beth. It's Kirsty. She's met this boy, and I'm just not happy about it.'

'Why not? What's wrong with him?'

Liz shrugged. 'Oh, I don't know. He seems a nice enough lad in his way. I just wish I could say the same about those he hangs out with.'

'Troublemakers, you think?'

'I can't say for sure. They may be quite innocent, but you hear such stories nowadays, about drugs and all that.'

'Yes, it's scary. But if you try laying down the law to your kids, they just think you're fussing. It makes them all the more determined to do their own thing.'

'Exactly. I know I have to give Kirsty her space, and I'm probably being ridiculously overprotective, but I can't help feeling anxious about what she might be getting into.'

Beth nodded sympathetically. 'Tell me about it! It was the same with my two a couple of years back – the worry almost drove us to distraction – but they've settled down OK now. Don't you fret about Kirsty, she's a good kid. I know it's easy for me to say, but I can't see her doing anything daft.'

'You're probably right,' sighed Liz, 'but I wish I could be sure.'

'She'll be fine,' soothed Beth. 'You'll see.'

Discussion points

- According to Paul in Romans 8:28, all things work together for good with those who love God. In what ways do you think that's true? Should this, then, be the attitude we have as Christians? How far does it differ from wishful thinking or naïve optimism?

- In what areas of life should we confidently expect God's blessing? In what areas *shouldn't* we?
- Have there been setbacks, problems or low points in your life that have ultimately brought you blessing or that God has worked through? What were these and what did you learn through them?

Scenario 4

Justin clutched hold of the present, trembling with excitement. It had seemed an eternity, counting down the long days to Christmas, but at last the waiting was over. No more guessing what the present might be. No more fingering or shaking the package, trying to work out what was inside or to read the label through the paper. He was about to see for himself.

But then he paused, hardly daring to continue. He knew what he wanted and had dropped endless hints to his parents in case they had any doubts on that score, but what if they hadn't listened, or couldn't afford it, or had simply decided on something else – clothes perhaps, or something for school – what then?

No, he was being silly. Whatever they'd bought he was bound to like it, and anyway it was probably exactly what he wanted – the brand new *Battle-zone* PlayStation game that was all the rage among his mates.

'Come on, Justin,' said his mum eagerly. 'Aren't you going to open it?'

He looked up at his parents' expectant faces, catching the doting look in their eyes, and suddenly he knew that, whatever else, he wouldn't be disappointed. With a bold flourish he whipped off the paper – and then gasped in delight. It was indeed the game he'd longed for, but, more than that, it was the deluxe version, with two other games into the bargain – more than he'd dared to dream.

'Brill!' he shouted. 'Thanks, Mum, thanks, Dad, it's well cool!'

His dad beamed happily. 'So then, Son, you reckon it was worth waiting for?'

'Worth it, Dad?' laughed Justin. 'Too right it was!'

Discussion points

- Have there been times in life generally when your wildest hopes were exceeded? What were they? How did you feel?
- What do you believe God holds in store in terms of eternity? Do you have any conception of heaven and eternal life? How far is it possible for people to get their heads round such things? Are you confident that hope will not disappoint you? On what is that faith based?
- In what ways have God's blessings in *this* life surprised you? Have there been times when he's understood your needs better than you did yourself, or done for you more than you could ever ask or imagine?

Prayer

Lord, whose way is perfect,
  help me always to trust in your goodness,
  that walking with you
  and following you in all simplicity,
  I may possess a quiet and contented mind
  and may cast all care on you,
  for you care for me.
Amen.

Christina Rossetti (1830–1894)

Food for thought

Consider the following proverbs and quotations. Which do you find most helpful? What are their strengths and weaknesses? Do you agree or disagree with the point they're making?

- All things come to those who wait. (Traditional)
- The future belongs to those who know how to wait. (Russian)

- Time is a threefold present: the present as we experience it, the past as a present memory and the future as a present expectation. (Augustine of Hippo)
- Most men prefer and strive for the present, we for the future. (St Ambrose)
- He who has no vision of eternity will never get a true hold of time. (Thomas Carlyle)

Prayer

God of new beginnings,
remind us of all you have done
and open our hearts to all you yet hold in store.
Teach us to wait in hope,
to look forward with expectation.

At the start of each day,
awaken us to the possibilities it holds –
its potential for love, happiness, growth and service.
Teach us to wait in hope,
to look forward with expectation.

At whatever stage of life we find ourselves,
remind us there is more to experience,
more to enjoy
and more to discover.
Teach us to wait in hope,
to look forward with expectation.

At whatever stage we have reached in discipleship,
remind us you have new blessings to impart,
new insights to share,
new opportunities to unfold,
new life to offer.

Teach us to wait in hope,
to look forward with expectation.

At times of sorrow or difficulty,
help us still to look forward,
assured of laughter after tears,
light after darkness,
pleasure after pain
and life after death.
Teach us to wait in hope,
to look forward with expectation.

At any and every moment,
help us to anticipate the future,
trusting that whatever joys may have been,
still you hold the best in store.
Teach us to wait in hope,
to look forward with expectation.
Amen.

Completing the picture

Below are some biblical verses about waiting and trust. Reflect on them for a time quietly together, and then discuss any further thoughts arising from them.

- For the moment we see but a blurred image in a mirror, then we shall see face to face; now I see only in part, but then I will fully know, just as I am fully known. (1 Corinthians 13:12)
- When you first heard the word of truth, the Good News, you heard also about the hope it offers, your faith and love being based on that hope, which is kept safe for you in heaven. (Colossians 1:5)

- We know that all things work together for good with those who love God, who have been called according to his purpose . . . I am convinced that nothing can separate us from his love in Christ. Neither death nor life, nor angels nor demons, nor the present nor the future, nor any powers, nor height nor depth nor anything else in all creation will ever be able to separate us from the love of God that is ours through Jesus Christ our Lord. (Romans 8:28, 38, 39)
- We rejoice in our present suffering because we know that suffering creates endurance, and endurance creates fortitude, and fortitude creates hope, and hope does not disappoint us, for through his Holy Spirit – his gift to us – God has poured his love liberally into our hearts. (Romans 5:4, 5)

Blessing

To him who by his power at work within us
is able to achieve inestimably more
than anything we can ask or even dream of,
to him be glory in the Church and in Christ Jesus
in this and every generation,
now and always.
Amen.

Ephesians 3:20, 21

Session 5
No waiting – grasping the moment

Theme

Waiting is right sometimes but not always. On occasions we must be ready to act rather than put off the moment.

Opening prayer

Too late came I to love you, O Beauty both ancient and ever new;
  too late came I to love you.
Behold! you were within me,
  and I was out of myself searching for you.
You, indeed, were with me, but I was not with you.
You called to me; yes, you even broke open my deafness.
Your beams shined unto me and cast away my blindness.
You blew upon me, and I drew in my breath and panted after you.
I tasted you, and now I hunger and thirst for you.
You touched me, and I ever burn again to enjoy your peace.
Amen.

St Augustine of Hippo (354–430)

Setting the scene

If you can help your neighbours now, never ask them to wait until tomorrow. If you wait for the wind and weather to be exactly right, you'll never plant or harvest anything. (Proverbs 3:28; Ecclesiastes 11:4)

He said to another man, 'Follow me', but the man answered, 'Sir, allow me first to return and bury my father.' 'Leave the dead to bury their own dead,' answered Jesus. 'You go instead and announce the kingdom of God.' Somebody else said, 'I'll follow you, sir; but permit me first to say my farewells to my family.' 'Anyone who begins to plough,' replied Jesus, 'only to keep looking back is not suited for the kingdom of God.' (Luke 9:59-62)

Activity

Divide into small groups and play the card game Snap a few times. Afterwards, reflect informally on what this game has to teach us about life: for example, about seizing the moment, staying alert to possibilities, responding while we can.

Introduction

Advent, as we have seen, is a time for waiting, for anticipating the future God holds in store. But waiting implies there's a reason for doing so – that we wait with a definite goal in mind, a specific objective, and that when this materialises we will grasp the moment. We don't wait for a bus, for example, only to turn our backs on it when it arrives and wait for another. Nor do we wait for a diagnosis only to ignore it. And so we could go on. There comes a time when our patience is rewarded and we spring into action, glad to wait no longer.

Sadly, though, that doesn't always happen. We may grow so tired of waiting that we give up, or perhaps allow our attention to be distracted, so that we miss what it was we were waiting for. We may wait for the wrong thing and thus find it never comes. We may hesitate at just the wrong moment, allowing what we were waiting for to pass us by. Or we may simply use hopes of some hazy future as an excuse to avoid action in the present. In other words, waiting has its dangers. Just as it would be foolhardy to park a car on an urban freeway, so in life and faith there are times when it's equally foolish to stand still; times when we should be moving on rather than staying in the same place. Advent speaks of this too, issuing alongside its call to wait an uncompromising challenge: 'NO WAITING!'

The contradiction is more apparent than real, not least because much of the waiting Advent speaks of has already been brought to an end through the life, death and resurrection of Christ. God's promise to Abraham of a son through whom all the earth would be blessed has been fulfilled. So also has his promise of the Messiah, the one who would usher in the dawn of God's kingdom. So again has his promise to send his Spirit, to teach, guide, inspire and empower. It's true that we still see and know only in part. It's true that, like the Apostle Paul, we still press on towards the goal God has set before us. And it's true that we still wait for the fulfilment of his purpose, our hope being not on earth but in heaven. Despite all this, God has acted decisively in human history, demonstrating his love and extending his mercy, and having done so he asks for a response, inviting us to receive his gift and share his life. We can put it off if we want to, but that is to deny ourselves the blessing he longs to share. His message, and one as central to Advent as any other, is that spelt out above: 'NO WAITING!' And it's precisely this response that we see illustrated in the two readings that follow.

Exploring the Scriptures

Luke 2:8-16

There were shepherds in that area, living in the fields and keeping watch over their flock during the night. Suddenly, an angel of the Lord appeared to them, and the glory of the Lord shone around them, and they were overcome with terror. However, the angel said to them, 'There's nothing to be frightened of; for see – I am bringing you good news of great joy that is for all people: today a Saviour has been born to you in the city of David, who is Christ the Lord. Let this be a sign to you: you will find a child swaddled in strips of cloth and lying in a manger.' All at once, there was with the angel rank on rank of other heavenly beings, praising God and saying, 'Glory to God in the highest heaven, and peace on earth among all on whom his favour rests!' When the angels had departed and returned to heaven, the shepherds said to each other, 'Let us go, then, to Bethlehem and see this event that has taken place, which the Lord has made known to us.' So they came with haste, and found Mary and Joseph, and the baby lying in a manger.

Acts 8:30, 31, 34-36

Running up to the chariot, Philip heard [the eunuch] reading Isaiah the prophet, so he asked him, 'Do you understand these words you're reading?' The eunuch answered, 'How can I possibly do that unless someone explains them to me?' And he urged Philip to come up and sit with him. The eunuch asked Philip, 'Tell me, of whom is the prophet talking here? Does he refer to himself or someone else?' Then Philip, beginning with that passage of scripture, talked to him about Jesus. As they were going on their way, they came to some water, and immediately the eunuch said, 'Look, here is water. What is there to stop me from being baptised?'

Enlarging the picture

The shepherds and the Ethiopian eunuch in the passages above shared one thing in common – they were all eager to respond. Not for them a long period of heart searching, agonising over what they should or shouldn't do. Not for them shilly-shallying over the fine print, weighing up the pros and cons before dipping their foot into the water. They'd heard good news and wanted to respond as quickly as they could. Why wait, why hang around, they reasoned? What could be gained through any delay? Here was something special, wonderful, and they wanted to be part of it.

Advent calls us in turn to respond to God's coming in Christ; to make up our minds what his living, dying and rising means for us today. It calls us to commit our lives to him, to find forgiveness and to receive new life. And it calls us to more besides, as we shall explore in the following scenarios.

Scenario 1

Sarah looked anxiously at her husband as another fit of coughing racked his frail body. He didn't sound well, or look it either. 'Harry, dear,' she said, 'I really think you should go to the doctor and get that cough checked out.'

Harry shrugged impatiently. 'It's nothing. Just some wretched bug I picked up somewhere.'

'But, Harry, it's been months now, and you keep saying that. When's it going to improve?'

'Don't fuss, woman!'

'I can't help it. What if it's something serious?'

'Here we go again,' sighed her husband. 'Honestly, it's just a cough.'

'You don't *know* that! And if it's anything worse, God forbid, then you can't afford to delay.'

Harry snorted. 'Talk about making a mountain out of a molehill. It's nothing, I tell you.'

'Oh, Harry,' answered his wife, a sob breaking into her voice, 'I want to believe that as much as you, but isn't it worth making sure? Please, darling, to humour me if nothing else, get it looked at.'

'Tell you what,' said Harry. 'If it's not better in a couple of weeks, I'll go then – I promise. How does that sound?'

Sarah sighed, knowing it was useless to argue. 'If you say so, love, but I wish you'd go today. Don't leave it too late, love, I'm begging you.'

Discussion points

- What caused Harry to delay seeing the doctor? Have you delayed doing things for similar reasons?

- What other excuses have you come up with over the years for avoiding what you'd rather not do? What were your real reasons?
- Have the factors discussed above prevented you from taking decisions or taking on challenges to which you believe God is calling you?

Scenario 2

'It's a girl, Mum – a beautiful daughter!'

Natasha's mum almost dropped the phone in her excitement. 'Oh, darling, that's wonderful. I'm so happy for you!'

'Thanks, Mum.'

'And how about you, Tasha, are you OK?'

'I'm fine, Mum. It wasn't easy, but it was worth it. She's so incredible; we're both over the moon!'

'I can't wait to see her,' said her mum. 'Do you think you'll feel up to a visit tomorrow?'

'Of course, Mum, come as soon as you want – now, if you like.'

'Oh, I couldn't do that, love; you must be exhausted.'

'Not too tired to see you, though. This is special for *you* as well as us, remember, and we want you to be part of it.'

'Thanks, love, just so long as I won't be in the way.'

'There's no chance of that.'

'You're quite sure?' said her mother.

'Positive, Mum! Now get yourself down here and stop fussing.'

Megan smiled. 'I will, darling. I'll come straightaway. Oh Tash, I'm so excited. Congratulations again, and see you soon!'

Discussion points

- Natasha's mum wanted to share in a special moment but, for what seemed good reasons, she was ready to put it off. Have there been times when you argued yourself out of something, only to regret it afterwards? What were they and what were your reasons?
- What reasons might the shepherds have come up with for not going to Bethlehem, or the Ethiopian eunuch for not being

baptised? Are you putting off responding to God for what look like the best of reasons? Are they really such good reasons after all, important enough to justify postponing a decision?

- Natasha's mum saw problems that weren't there, feeling unsure of the welcome she'd receive. Do you make that mistake sometimes in relation to God, imagining there are barriers keeping you apart? Do you see him as a God always ready to welcome, or is your picture different?

Scenario 3

'Hello, Graham, I didn't expect to see you here. It *is* Graham, isn't it?'

'Yes, it is. And *you* . . . don't tell me . . . not Will Johnson, surely?'

'I've not changed that much, then! Bit less hair, I expect, and a hint more padding round the middle.'

'That's one way of putting it,' grinned Graham. 'You look well.'

'Thanks, can't complain. So, what are you doing with yourself now?'

'I'm at the bank in the high street. Do you remember the place?'

'I'll say I do. I had an interview there myself, remember, around the same time as you. But surely you're not still there?'

'I'm afraid so. Always meant to move on, or at least move up, but somehow it never happened.'

'You tried, though?'

'Well, no, I didn't eventually. I should have taken more exams, looked for promotion, but I kept putting it off, telling myself there'd be time for that later, until suddenly there wasn't time after all.'

'So you're stuck where you are, then?'

'Yep, same place, same job. I could do with a change, believe me, but I've only myself to blame. I dithered too long instead of going for it while I had the chance.'

Will paused, looking thoughtful. 'Tell you what,' he said at length. 'I've a business of my own – pretty successful too – and we're looking to expand at the moment. If you're interested, come along for an interview tomorrow. Here's my card.'

Graham gazed at it in disbelief. 'Are you serious?'

'Sure.'

'Thanks, mate. I don't know what to say!'

'No need for thanks,' said Will. 'I've not offered you a job yet, remember, but if you're up to it, you'll be doing us both a favour.'

'Tomorrow it is, then,' said Graham, shaking Will's hand enthusiastically. 'What time?'

'Let's say ten-thirty,' answered Will. He walked away, then swung round with a smile. 'Oh, by the way, don't leave it too late.'

Discussion points

- What's the danger of putting something off until tomorrow? Can you think of examples of this from personal experience? Are there things you're putting off now?
- Is there a danger as Christians, perhaps also as a church, of getting stuck in a rut? What might cause this? How can we prevent it?
- How far have you progressed in your faith? Is it stronger than when you first became a Christian or have you lost your sense of purpose? In what way has your faith changed over the years and changed *you* with it?

Scenario 4

'Hey, Mike, have you been to the sale yet? There are some great bargains!'

'No, I don't think I'll bother. I bet they've marked the prices up before putting them down again. That's what they always do.'

'Not this time they haven't. Just look at this: a widescreen TV for less than two hundred quid, and a laptop for three hundred and fifty. Not bad, eh?'

'Not bad at all,' agreed Mike. 'Maybe I *will* pop down some time, after all.'

'You'd better hurry. They're selling out fast and the sale ends tomorrow.'

'Pull the other one,' answered Mike. 'There's always a sale on down there; it's just a ploy to keep the customers coming in.'

'I wouldn't be too sure of that. They've sold out of lots of stuff already.'

'Oh well, I'll take my chance. I want to watch the golf on telly tomorrow. Maybe I'll try next week.'

Jesse shrugged. 'Have it your way, but if you're too late, don't say I didn't warn you.'

Discussion points

- Have there been times when you've missed opportunities through being too slow to grasp them? What were they? What made you delay?
- Did you put off making a decision before you first became a Christian or did you respond immediately? If the former, what factors held you back? Did you eventually resolve the issues or simply feel that you had to take the plunge?
- Have there been times when you've resolved to work at your discipleship, spend more time in prayer, read the Bible more often, get more involved in the life of your fellowship, and so on, yet never quite got round to it? What's stopping you? Are the things you're doing instead really so important, or are you depriving yourself of what matters most of all?

Prayer

O Lord my God,
take away from me all that blocks my way to you;
give me all that speeds me towards you;
rescue me from myself,
and give me as your own to yourself.
Amen.

St Nicholas von Flüe (1417–1487)

Food for thought

Consider the following proverbs and quotations. Which do you find most helpful? What are their strengths and weaknesses? Do you agree or disagree with the point they're making?

- He who hesitates is lost. (Traditional)
- Strike while the iron is hot. (Traditional)
- Tomorrow never comes. (Traditional)
- One today is worth two tomorrows. (Traditional)
- Procrastination is the thief of time. (Traditional)
- Never put off till tomorrow what you can do today. (Traditional)
- No time like the present. (Traditional)
- One of these days is none of these days. (Traditional)
- Opportunity seldom knocks twice. (Traditional)
- All the treasures of earth cannot bring back one lost moment. (French)

Prayer

Loving God,
remind us that there is a time to wait and a time to act,
a time for patience and a time for seizing the moment.
Help us to know the difference.

When you call us to greater commitment,
to show in our lives what we profess with our lips,
help us to hear your voice
and to answer.

When you call us to repentance,
to acknowledge our faults and turn from them,
help us to hear your voice
and to answer.

When you call us to service,
putting the needs of others before our own,
giving to you through giving to them,
help us to hear your voice
and to answer.

When you call us to reflection,
to spend time alone with you,
seeking your will and guidance,
help us to hear your voice
and to answer.

When you call us to decisions,
to choices about our priorities and the way we live,
help us to hear your voice
and to answer.

Whatever your call,
whatever your will,
when the moment of truth comes,
and the time for wavering is over,
help us to hear your voice
and to answer.
Amen.

Completing the picture

Below are some biblical verses about grasping the moment. Reflect on them quietly together, and then discuss any further thoughts arising from them.

- So then, why wait any longer? Get up, pray to him, be baptised, and have your sins washed away. (Acts 22:16)
- Look, I present you today with a straight choice between life and death, good and evil. If you obey the commandments of the Lord

your God that I am giving you today – loving the Lord God, following his ways and keeping his commandments, instructions and laws – then you will live and prosper, and the Lord God will bless you in the land you are about to take possession of. (Deuteronomy 30:15, 16)

- If you would rather not serve the Lord, then choose this day whom you will serve . . . but as for me and my household, we will serve the Lord. (Joshua 24:15)
- It is time for you to awake from sleep, for the moment of salvation is nearer now than when we first came to faith. Night-time is almost over, daybreak is nearly here, so let us have nothing more to do with what belongs to darkness, taking up instead the armour of light. Let us behave as befits those who live in the full light of day – no promiscuity or getting drunk, no immoral or indecent behaviour, no hostility or envy. Let us clothe ourselves rather with the Lord Jesus Christ, and pander no longer to our earthly desires. (Romans 13:11b-14)
- I know the truth about you: that though you are reputedly alive, in actual fact you are dead, what you have done being far from perfect in the eyes of God. Wake up then, and shore up what you still have before it perishes entirely. Remember, then, what you have received and heard; observe it and turn from your old ways. If you fail to awake, I will come upon you like a thief at an hour you will have no way of knowing. (Revelation 3:1b-3)

A final word

Time is:
too slow for those who wait,
too swift for those who fear,
too long for those who grieve,
too short for those who rejoice;
but for those who love, time is eternity.

Henry Van Dyke (1852–1933)

Blessing

Show us what you would have us do, Lord,
and give us the courage to do it.
Equip us with the faith, vision and commitment we need
to respond to your call,
and in grasping the moment
may we grasp more firmly hold of you.
Amen.